# Success With
# Math Tests

**SCHOLASTIC**

Editor: Ourania Papacharalambous
Educational consultant: Michael Priestley
Cover design by Tannaz Fassihi; cover illustration by Kevin Zimmer
Interior design by Michelle H. Kim
Interior illustrations by Kate Flanagan, Doug Jones (3)

ISBN 978-1-338-79847-0
Scholastic Inc., 557 Broadway, New York, NY 10012
Copyright © 2022 Scholastic Inc.
All rights reserved. Printed in the U.S.A.
First printing, January 2022

1 2 3 4 5 6 7 8 9 10    40    29 28 27 26 25 24 23 22

# TABLE OF CONTENTS

# INTRODUCTION

In this book, you will find eight Practice Tests designed to help students prepare to take standardized tests. Each test has multiple-choice items that closely resemble the kinds of questions students will have to answer on "real" tests. Each part of the test will take 30–40 minutes for students to complete.

The math skills measured in these tests and the types of questions are based on detailed analyses and correlations with many widely used standardized tests and curriculum standards.

## How to Use the Tests

Tell students how much time they will have to complete the test. Encourage them to work quickly and carefully and to keep track of the remaining time—just as they would in a real testing session. You may have students mark their answers directly on the test pages, or you may have them use a copy of the **Answer Sheet**. A copy of the answer sheet appears at the end of each test. The answer sheet will help students become accustomed to filling in bubbles on a real test. It may also make the tests easier for you to score.

We do not recommend the use of calculators. For Practice Tests 2 and 6, students will need an inch ruler and a centimeter ruler to answer some of the questions.

At the back of this book, you will find **Tested Skills** charts and **Answer Keys** for the eight Practice Tests. The Tested Skills charts list the skills measured in each test and the test questions that measure each skill. These charts may be helpful to you in determining what kinds of questions students answered incorrectly, what skills they may be having trouble with, and who may need further instruction in particular skills. To score a Practice Test, refer to the Answer Key for that test. The Answer Key lists the correct response to each question.

To score a Practice Test, go through the test and mark each question answered correctly. Add the total number of questions answered correctly to find the student's test score. To find a percentage score, divide the number answered correctly by the total number of questions. For example, the percentage score for a student who answers 20 out of 25 questions correctly is 20 ÷ 25 = 0.80, or 80%. You might want to have students correct their own tests. This will give them a chance to see where they made mistakes and what they need to do to improve their scores on the next test.

On the next page of this book, you will find **Test-Taking Tips**. You may want to share these tips and strategies with students before they begin working on the Practice Tests.

# TEST-TAKING TIPS: MATHEMATICS

**1** For each part of the test, read the directions carefully so you know what to do. Then, read the directions again—just to make sure.

**2** Look for key words and phrases to help you decide what each question is asking and what kind of computation you need to do. Examples of key words: *less than*, *greatest*, *least*, *farther*, *longest*, *divided equally*.

**3** To help solve a problem, write a number sentence or equation.

**4** Use scrap paper (or extra space on the test page) to write down the numbers and information you need to solve a problem.

**5** If a question has a picture or diagram, study it carefully. Draw your own picture or diagram if it will help you solve a problem.

**6** Try to solve each problem before you look at the answer choices. (In some tests, the correct answer may not be given, so you will want to be sure of your answer. In these Practice Tests, some of the Math questions use "NG" for "Not Given.")

**7** Check your work carefully before you finish. (For many questions, you can check your answer by working backwards to see if the numbers work out correctly.)

**8** If you are not sure which answer is correct, cross out every answer that you know is wrong. Then, make your best guess.

**9** To complete a number sentence or equation, try all the answer choices until you find the one that works.

**10** When working with fractions, always reduce (or rename) the fractions to their lowest parts. When working with decimals, keep the decimal points lined up correctly.

## Practice Test 1: Numeration and Number Concepts

**Directions. Choose the best answer to each question. Mark your answer.**

**1** The population of a major U.S. city was 1,198,064. How should this number be written in words?

&#9398; one million nineteen thousand eight hundred sixty-four

&#9399; one million one hundred ninety-eight thousand sixty-four

&#9400; one million one hundred ninety-eight thousand six hundred forty

&#9401; one billion one hundred ninety-eight million sixty-four

**2** An amusement park had four million seven hundred thousand visitors last year. How should that be written in numerals?

&#9398; 4,000,700

&#9399; 4,070,000

&#9400; 4,700,000

&#9401; 4,007,000

**3** $5^4 =$

&#9398; 5 x 4

&#9399; 5 x 5 x 4

&#9400; 5 x 4 x 5 x 4

&#9401; 5 x 5 x 5 x 5

**4** The chart lists the population of four African countries in 2020.

| Country | Population |
|---------|-----------|
| Malawi | 19,129,952 |
| Mali | 20,250,833 |
| Mozambique | 32,198,611 |
| Niger | 32,198,611 |

Which country had the smallest population?

&#9398; Malawi

&#9399; Mali

&#9400; Mozambique

&#9401; Niger

**5** This chart shows the average winter temperature over four days.

| Day | Average Tempurature |
|-----|---------------------|
| Sunday | -12°F |
| Monday | 0°F |
| Tuesday | -4°F |
| Wednesday | 6°F |

Which day had the lowest average temperature?

&#9398; Sunday     &#9400; Tuesday

&#9399; Monday     &#9401; Wednesday

**GO ON** ➡

# Practice Test 1 (continued)

**6** This chart lists the number of events played and the official earnings for the leading players in ladies golf for 2021.

| Player | Events | Earnings |
|---|---|---|
| Nelly Korda | 13 | $1,856,649 |
| Yuka Saso | 4 | $1,181,642 |
| Lydia Ko | 15 | $1,169,962 |
| Patty Tavatanakit | 12 | $1,022,212 |

Which list shows the players in order from most events played to least events played?

Ⓐ Korda, Saso, Ko, Tavatanakit

Ⓑ Ko, Korda, Tavatanakit, Saso

Ⓒ Tavatanakit, Ko, Saso, Korda

Ⓓ Saso, Ko, Korda, Tavatanakit

**7** The planet Mercury is about 35,000,000 miles from the sun. What is the value of the 5 in 35,000,000?

Ⓐ 5 million

Ⓑ 5 hundred thousand

Ⓒ 5 thousand

Ⓓ 5 hundred

**8** Which is an odd number?

Ⓐ 2390

Ⓑ 7702

Ⓒ 3475

Ⓓ 4806

**9** The average diameter of Jupiter is 88,846 miles. What is that number rounded to the nearest thousand?

Ⓐ 88,000

Ⓑ 88,800

Ⓒ 89,000

Ⓓ 89,800

**10** $4{,}000{,}000 + 30{,}000 + 8000 + 20 =$

Ⓐ 4,380,020

Ⓑ 4,308,200

Ⓒ 4,038,020

Ⓓ 4,030,820

**11** $3.4 \times 10^2 =$

Ⓐ 304

Ⓑ 340

Ⓒ 3400

Ⓓ 34,000

**12** Janice created this number pattern.

2, 5, 11, 23, _____

If this pattern continues, what number should come next?

Ⓐ 24

Ⓑ 46

Ⓒ 47

Ⓓ 48

GO ON

## Practice Test 1 *(continued)*

**13** Which is a prime number?

Ⓐ 9

Ⓑ 10

Ⓒ 14

Ⓓ 17

**14** Which numbers are both factors of 39?

Ⓐ 6, 7

Ⓑ 3, 13

Ⓒ 5, 8

Ⓓ 4, 9

**15** The Acme Trucking Company has three vans. Last year, Van A was driven 24,725 miles. Van B was driven 19,620 miles. Van C was driven 30,480 miles. <u>About</u> how many miles did the three vans travel all together?

Ⓐ 40,000 miles

Ⓑ 60,000 miles

Ⓒ 75,000 miles

Ⓓ 100,000 miles

**16** A stadium in City A holds 104,895 people. A stadium in City B holds 85,107 people. <u>About</u> how many more people does the stadium in City A hold?

Ⓐ 20,000

Ⓑ 15,000

Ⓒ 10,000

Ⓓ 5000

**17** Look at the number line.

The arrow is pointing to what number on the number line?

Ⓐ −160

Ⓑ −140

Ⓒ −120

Ⓓ −40

**18** What fractional part of the figure is shaded?

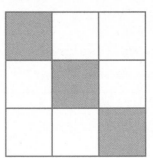

Ⓐ $\frac{1}{2}$

Ⓑ $\frac{1}{3}$

Ⓒ $\frac{1}{4}$

Ⓓ $\frac{1}{5}$

**GO ON**

# Practice Test 1 *(continued)*

**19** Of the 120 cars in a parking lot, 24 are blue. What fractional part of the cars in the lot are blue?

Ⓐ $\frac{1}{5}$

Ⓑ $\frac{1}{3}$

Ⓒ $\frac{1}{4}$

Ⓓ $\frac{1}{6}$

**20** The chart shows the length of the winning triple jump in four Summer Olympics.

| Year | Athlete | Length |
|------|---------|--------|
| 2008 | N. Évora | 17.31m |
| 2012 | C. Taylor | 17.81m |
| 2016 | C. Taylor | 17.86m |
| 2020 | P. Pichardo | 17.98m |

Who had the longest triple jump?

Ⓐ N. Evora in 2008

Ⓑ C. Taylor in 2012

Ⓒ C. Taylor in 2016

Ⓓ P. Pichardo in 2020

**21** Which number sentence is true?

Ⓐ $1 + \frac{1}{2} = \frac{2}{2}$

Ⓑ $\frac{1}{2} \times 0 = 0$

Ⓒ $\frac{3}{4} \times 1 = 1$

Ⓓ $\frac{1}{2} \times \frac{3}{4} = \frac{1}{4} \times \frac{2}{3}$

**22** Which is the least amount?

Ⓐ $\frac{1}{4}$ cup

Ⓑ $\frac{1}{3}$ cup

Ⓒ $\frac{1}{6}$ cup

Ⓓ $\frac{1}{8}$ cup

**23** Which fraction is another name for $3\frac{1}{2}$?

Ⓐ $\frac{7}{2}$

Ⓑ $\frac{4}{2}$

Ⓒ $\frac{5}{2}$

Ⓓ $\frac{6}{2}$

**24** $\frac{45}{100}$

Ⓐ 4.5

Ⓑ 4.05

Ⓒ 0.45

Ⓓ 0.045

**25** Look at the number line.

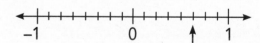

The arrow is pointing to what number on the number line?

Ⓐ $\frac{1}{2}$

Ⓑ $\frac{2}{3}$

Ⓒ $\frac{5}{8}$

Ⓓ $\frac{3}{8}$

STOP

# Answer Sheet

Student Name _____ Grade _____

Teacher Name _____ Date _____

## MATHEMATICS

| | | |
|---|---|---|
| 1 Ⓐ Ⓑ Ⓒ Ⓓ Ⓔ | 11 Ⓐ Ⓑ Ⓒ Ⓓ Ⓔ | 21 Ⓐ Ⓑ Ⓒ Ⓓ Ⓔ |
| 2 Ⓐ Ⓑ Ⓒ Ⓓ Ⓔ | 12 Ⓐ Ⓑ Ⓒ Ⓓ Ⓔ | 22 Ⓐ Ⓑ Ⓒ Ⓓ Ⓔ |
| 3 Ⓐ Ⓑ Ⓒ Ⓓ Ⓔ | 13 Ⓐ Ⓑ Ⓒ Ⓓ Ⓔ | 23 Ⓐ Ⓑ Ⓒ Ⓓ Ⓔ |
| 4 Ⓐ Ⓑ Ⓒ Ⓓ Ⓔ | 14 Ⓐ Ⓑ Ⓒ Ⓓ Ⓔ | 24 Ⓐ Ⓑ Ⓒ Ⓓ Ⓔ |
| 5 Ⓐ Ⓑ Ⓒ Ⓓ Ⓔ | 15 Ⓐ Ⓑ Ⓒ Ⓓ Ⓔ | 25 Ⓐ Ⓑ Ⓒ Ⓓ Ⓔ |
| 6 Ⓐ Ⓑ Ⓒ Ⓓ Ⓔ | 16 Ⓐ Ⓑ Ⓒ Ⓓ Ⓔ | 26 Ⓐ Ⓑ Ⓒ Ⓓ Ⓔ |
| 7 Ⓐ Ⓑ Ⓒ Ⓓ Ⓔ | 17 Ⓐ Ⓑ Ⓒ Ⓓ Ⓔ | 27 Ⓐ Ⓑ Ⓒ Ⓓ Ⓔ |
| 8 Ⓐ Ⓑ Ⓒ Ⓓ Ⓔ | 18 Ⓐ Ⓑ Ⓒ Ⓓ Ⓔ | 28 Ⓐ Ⓑ Ⓒ Ⓓ Ⓔ |
| 9 Ⓐ Ⓑ Ⓒ Ⓓ Ⓔ | 19 Ⓐ Ⓑ Ⓒ Ⓓ Ⓔ | 29 Ⓐ Ⓑ Ⓒ Ⓓ Ⓔ |
| 10 Ⓐ Ⓑ Ⓒ Ⓓ Ⓔ | 20 Ⓐ Ⓑ Ⓒ Ⓓ Ⓔ | 30 Ⓐ Ⓑ Ⓒ Ⓓ Ⓔ |

# Practice Test 2: Geometry and Measurement

**Directions. Choose the best answer to each question. Mark your answer.**

**1** Carlin Road is 1.2 kilometers long. How many meters is that?

Ⓐ 12,000

Ⓑ 1200

Ⓒ 120

Ⓓ 12

**2** Which figure has 6 edges?

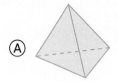 Ⓐ

 Ⓒ

 Ⓑ

 Ⓓ

**3** What is the perimeter of this figure? Use your inch ruler.

Ⓐ $3\frac{3}{4}$ in.

Ⓑ 5 in.

Ⓒ $6\frac{1}{4}$ in.

Ⓓ $7\frac{1}{2}$ in.

**4** Point O is at the center of this circle. Which line segment is a radius of the circle?

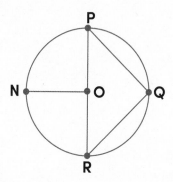

Ⓐ $\overline{NO}$

Ⓑ $\overline{QR}$

Ⓒ $\overline{PQ}$

Ⓓ $\overline{PR}$

**5** Which figure shows a line of symmetry?

 Ⓐ

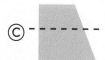 Ⓒ

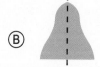 Ⓑ

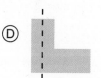 Ⓓ

GO ON

# Practice Test 2 (continued)

**6** Which figure is congruent to Figure A?

Figure A

Ⓐ 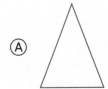    Ⓒ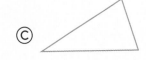

Ⓑ 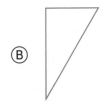    Ⓓ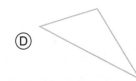

**7** Mr. Kelly put $8\frac{1}{2}$ gallons of gasoline in his car. How many quarts is that?

Ⓐ 17 qt
Ⓑ 24 qt
Ⓒ 32 qt
Ⓓ 34 qt

**8** Which unit should be used to measure the weight of a bag of potato chips?

Ⓐ pounds
Ⓑ cups
Ⓒ ounces
Ⓓ inches

**9** A pilot flew 1950 miles on Monday, 2110 miles on Tuesday, and 984 miles on Wednesday. <u>About</u> how many miles did she fly in all?

Ⓐ 3000
Ⓑ 4000
Ⓒ 5000
Ⓓ 6000

**10** A paving stone weighs $9\frac{3}{4}$ pounds. <u>About</u> how much do 32 paving stones weigh?

Ⓐ 200 lb
Ⓑ 300 lb
Ⓒ 400 lb
Ⓓ 500 lb

**11** Which sign is an octogon?

Ⓐ 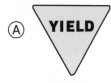    Ⓒ

Ⓑ     Ⓓ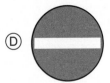

GO ON

# Practice Test 2 *(continued)*

The graph below shows the outside temperature recorded at different times on December 12. Use the graph to answer questions 12 and 13.

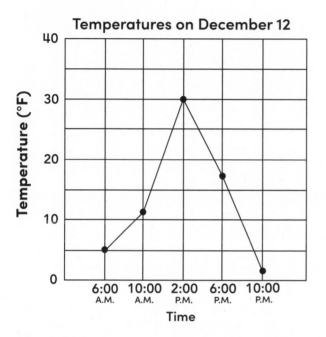

Temperatures on December 12

**12** What was the temperature at 2:00 P.M.?

Ⓐ 12°F

Ⓑ 18°F

Ⓒ 20°F

Ⓓ 30°F

**13** The lowest temperature was recorded at what time?

Ⓐ 6:00 A.M.

Ⓑ 10:00 A.M.

Ⓒ 6:00 P.M.

Ⓓ 10:00 P.M.

**14** <u>About</u> how much does a bag of potatoes weigh?

Ⓐ 10 pounds

Ⓑ 10 ounces

Ⓒ 10 grams

Ⓓ 10 tons

Use the figure below to answer questions 15 and 16.

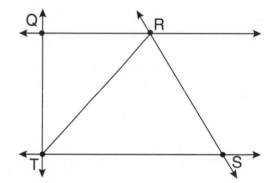

**15** Which is perpendicular to QR?

Ⓐ $\overline{RT}$

Ⓑ $\overleftrightarrow{RS}$

Ⓒ $\overrightarrow{TS}$

Ⓓ $\overleftrightarrow{QT}$

**16** Which angle is greater than 90 degrees?

Ⓐ ∠QTS

Ⓑ ∠QRS

Ⓒ ∠TSR

Ⓓ ∠TRS

GO ON

# Practice Test 2 *(continued)*

Use this map and an inch ruler to answer questions 17 and 18.

**Blue Lake State Park**

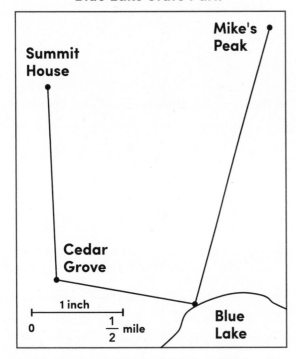

**17** What is the actual distance from Summit House to Cedar Grove?

(A) $\frac{1}{2}$ mile      (C) $1\frac{1}{2}$ miles

(B) 1 mile      (D) 2 miles

**18** Deanne hiked from Cedar Grove to Blue Lake and then to Mike's Peak. How far did she hike in all?

(A) $\frac{3}{4}$ mile      (C) 2 miles

(B) $1\frac{1}{2}$ miles      (D) $2\frac{1}{4}$ miles

**19** What is the volume of this figure?

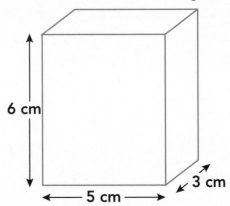

(A) 90 cm³

(B) 48 cm³

(C) 33 cm³

(D) 14 cm³

**20** This figure will be flipped over the line X.

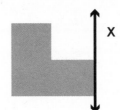

What will the figure look like after it has been flipped?

STOP

# Answer Sheet

Student Name _____     Grade _____

Teacher Name _____     Date _____

## MATHEMATICS

| | | |
|---|---|---|
| **1** Ⓐ Ⓑ Ⓒ Ⓓ Ⓔ | **11** Ⓐ Ⓑ Ⓒ Ⓓ Ⓔ | **21** Ⓐ Ⓑ Ⓒ Ⓓ Ⓔ |
| **2** Ⓐ Ⓑ Ⓒ Ⓓ Ⓔ | **12** Ⓐ Ⓑ Ⓒ Ⓓ Ⓔ | **22** Ⓐ Ⓑ Ⓒ Ⓓ Ⓔ |
| **3** Ⓐ Ⓑ Ⓒ Ⓓ Ⓔ | **13** Ⓐ Ⓑ Ⓒ Ⓓ Ⓔ | **23** Ⓐ Ⓑ Ⓒ Ⓓ Ⓔ |
| **4** Ⓐ Ⓑ Ⓒ Ⓓ Ⓔ | **14** Ⓐ Ⓑ Ⓒ Ⓓ Ⓔ | **24** Ⓐ Ⓑ Ⓒ Ⓓ Ⓔ |
| **5** Ⓐ Ⓑ Ⓒ Ⓓ Ⓔ | **15** Ⓐ Ⓑ Ⓒ Ⓓ Ⓔ | **25** Ⓐ Ⓑ Ⓒ Ⓓ Ⓔ |
| **6** Ⓐ Ⓑ Ⓒ Ⓓ Ⓔ | **16** Ⓐ Ⓑ Ⓒ Ⓓ Ⓔ | **26** Ⓐ Ⓑ Ⓒ Ⓓ Ⓔ |
| **7** Ⓐ Ⓑ Ⓒ Ⓓ Ⓔ | **17** Ⓐ Ⓑ Ⓒ Ⓓ Ⓔ | **27** Ⓐ Ⓑ Ⓒ Ⓓ Ⓔ |
| **8** Ⓐ Ⓑ Ⓒ Ⓓ Ⓔ | **18** Ⓐ Ⓑ Ⓒ Ⓓ Ⓔ | **28** Ⓐ Ⓑ Ⓒ Ⓓ Ⓔ |
| **9** Ⓐ Ⓑ Ⓒ Ⓓ Ⓔ | **19** Ⓐ Ⓑ Ⓒ Ⓓ Ⓔ | **29** Ⓐ Ⓑ Ⓒ Ⓓ Ⓔ |
| **10** Ⓐ Ⓑ Ⓒ Ⓓ Ⓔ | **20** Ⓐ Ⓑ Ⓒ Ⓓ Ⓔ | **30** Ⓐ Ⓑ Ⓒ Ⓓ Ⓔ |

# Practice Test 3: Problem Solving

**Directions. Choose the best answer to each question. Mark your answer. If the correct answer is *not given*, choose "NG."**

**1** A farmer made $1\frac{3}{4}$ pounds of goat cheese and $2\frac{1}{8}$ pounds of cheddar cheese. How much cheese did she make in all?

Ⓐ $3\frac{4}{12}$ lb

Ⓑ $3\frac{7}{8}$ lb

Ⓒ $3\frac{1}{2}$ lb

Ⓓ $3\frac{1}{4}$ lb

Ⓔ NG

**2** Shari bought these 3 books.

What is the total cost of these books?

Ⓐ $48.70

Ⓑ $53.55

Ⓒ $63.55

Ⓓ $63.65

Ⓔ NG

**3** Leon needs $82.00 for a new skateboard. He has saved $41.00. What percent of the total amount has he saved?

Ⓐ 60%

Ⓑ 50%

Ⓒ 41%

Ⓓ 30%

Ⓔ NG

**4** A pair of socks costs $4.95. A package of 3 pairs costs $12.00.

$4.95　　　　　　$12.00

How much do you save on 3 pairs of socks if you buy the package?

Ⓐ $2.85

Ⓑ $3.10

Ⓒ $9.90

Ⓓ $14.85

Ⓔ NG

**GO ON**

## Practice Test 3 *(continued)*

**5** Maureen wants to buy a winter coat that usually costs $50.00. The coat is on sale.

What is the sale price of the coat?

Ⓐ $15.00

Ⓑ $30.00

Ⓒ $35.00

Ⓓ $47.00

Ⓔ NG

**6** Justin was playing a game on his computer. He started playing at 1:15 P.M. and stopped playing at 3:40 P.M. How long did he play the game?

Ⓐ 2 hr 15 min

Ⓑ 2 hr 20 min

Ⓒ 2 hr 35 min

Ⓓ 3 hr 5 min

Ⓔ NG

**7** Mrs. Klein uses 12 cucumbers to make 3 jars of pickles. At this rate, how many cucumbers will she need to make 10 jars of pickles?

Ⓐ 24

Ⓑ 30

Ⓒ 32

Ⓓ 40

Ⓔ NG

**8** Candy bought a box of 50 books at a used book sale. Of those books, $\frac{3}{5}$ were paperbacks. How many paperback books did she buy?

Ⓐ 20

Ⓑ 25

Ⓒ 30

Ⓓ 35

Ⓔ NG

**9** On average, 162 cars go through the Coolidge Tunnel each hour. How many cars go through the tunnel in 12 hours?

Ⓐ 174

Ⓑ 486

Ⓒ 1944

Ⓓ 2044

Ⓔ NG

**GO ON**

# Practice Test 3 *(continued)*

**10** Five students sat in a row of seats in the auditorium. Bruce sat on one end. Grace sat between Bruce and Miles. Rita sat between Miles and Chad.

Who sat in the middle seat?

Ⓐ Rita

Ⓑ Grace

Ⓒ Chad

Ⓓ Miles

Ⓔ NG

**11** There are 98 boxes of seats at the football stadium. Each box has 12 seats. Which numbers would give the best estimate of the total number of box seats in the stadium?

Ⓐ 90 × 10

Ⓑ 90 × 20

Ⓒ 100 × 10

Ⓓ 100 × 20

**12** Steve earns $7.85 per hour at a fast food restaurant. <u>About</u> how much will he make in 42 hours?

Ⓐ $400

Ⓑ $360

Ⓒ $320

Ⓓ $280

**13** Mr. Guerrero gets 22 miles per gallon of gasoline in his truck. <u>About</u> how many miles can he go on 28 gallons of gasoline?

Ⓐ 400

Ⓑ 600

Ⓒ 800

Ⓓ 1000

**14** Mario baby-sat for a total of 28 hours last week. He earns $6.00 per hour for baby-sitting. Which question can you answer from this information?

Ⓐ How many different families did Mario baby-sit for?

Ⓑ What is the average amount of money Mario earns each week?

Ⓒ How many children did Mario baby-sit during the week?

Ⓓ How much money did Mario earn last week for baby-sitting?

Ⓔ NG

**GO ON**

# Practice Test 3 *(continued)*

**15** At a toy factory, workers pack 32 toys in a box for shipping. Which number sentence should you use to find how many boxes they will need to pack 2048 toys?

  (A) $2048 - 32 = \square$

  (B) $2048 \div 32 = \square$

  (C) $2048 \times 32 = \square$

  (D) $2048 + 32 = \square$

  (E) NG

**16** Mrs. Bryant counted 25 birds at her bird feeder one morning. Of those birds, 10 were blue jays. What percent of the birds were blue jays?

  (A) 10%

  (B) 25%

  (C) 30%

  (D) 45%

  (E) NG

**17** Duncan was baking bread and cake for a bake sale. He used $5\frac{1}{4}$ cups of flour for bread and $6\frac{3}{8}$ cups of flour for cake.

$5\frac{1}{4}$ cups

$6\frac{3}{8}$ cups

How much flour did he use in all?

  (A) $11\frac{4}{12}$ cups

  (B) $11\frac{1}{2}$ cups

  (C) $11\frac{5}{6}$ cups

  (D) $12\frac{1}{8}$ cups

  (E) NG

**18** Mr Chasse bought 4 tires at a tire sale.

TIRE SALE
$112.50 each

Including a sales tax of 6%, what was the total cost for the 4 tires?

  (A) $477.00

  (B) $474.00

  (C) $456.00

  (D) $450.00

  (E) NG

**STOP**

# Answer Sheet

Student Name _____   Grade _____

Teacher Name _____   Date _____

## MATHEMATICS

| | | |
|---|---|---|
| **1** Ⓐ Ⓑ Ⓒ Ⓓ Ⓔ | **11** Ⓐ Ⓑ Ⓒ Ⓓ Ⓔ | **21** Ⓐ Ⓑ Ⓒ Ⓓ Ⓔ |
| **2** Ⓐ Ⓑ Ⓒ Ⓓ Ⓔ | **12** Ⓐ Ⓑ Ⓒ Ⓓ Ⓔ | **22** Ⓐ Ⓑ Ⓒ Ⓓ Ⓔ |
| **3** Ⓐ Ⓑ Ⓒ Ⓓ Ⓔ | **13** Ⓐ Ⓑ Ⓒ Ⓓ Ⓔ | **23** Ⓐ Ⓑ Ⓒ Ⓓ Ⓔ |
| **4** Ⓐ Ⓑ Ⓒ Ⓓ Ⓔ | **14** Ⓐ Ⓑ Ⓒ Ⓓ Ⓔ | **24** Ⓐ Ⓑ Ⓒ Ⓓ Ⓔ |
| **5** Ⓐ Ⓑ Ⓒ Ⓓ Ⓔ | **15** Ⓐ Ⓑ Ⓒ Ⓓ Ⓔ | **25** Ⓐ Ⓑ Ⓒ Ⓓ Ⓔ |
| **6** Ⓐ Ⓑ Ⓒ Ⓓ Ⓔ | **16** Ⓐ Ⓑ Ⓒ Ⓓ Ⓔ | **26** Ⓐ Ⓑ Ⓒ Ⓓ Ⓔ |
| **7** Ⓐ Ⓑ Ⓒ Ⓓ Ⓔ | **17** Ⓐ Ⓑ Ⓒ Ⓓ Ⓔ | **27** Ⓐ Ⓑ Ⓒ Ⓓ Ⓔ |
| **8** Ⓐ Ⓑ Ⓒ Ⓓ Ⓔ | **18** Ⓐ Ⓑ Ⓒ Ⓓ Ⓔ | **28** Ⓐ Ⓑ Ⓒ Ⓓ Ⓔ |
| **9** Ⓐ Ⓑ Ⓒ Ⓓ Ⓔ | **19** Ⓐ Ⓑ Ⓒ Ⓓ Ⓔ | **29** Ⓐ Ⓑ Ⓒ Ⓓ Ⓔ |
| **10** Ⓐ Ⓑ Ⓒ Ⓓ Ⓔ | **20** Ⓐ Ⓑ Ⓒ Ⓓ Ⓔ | **30** Ⓐ Ⓑ Ⓒ Ⓓ Ⓔ |

# Practice Test 4: Computation

**Directions. Choose the best answer to each question. Mark your answer.
If the correct answer is *not given*, choose "NG."**

**1** 
$$\begin{array}{r} 58 \\ \times\ 43 \\ \hline \end{array}$$

(A) 406
(B) 2394
(C) 2494
(D) 2504
(E) NG

**2** 8)99

(A) 25
(B) 24 R7
(C) 24
(D) 2 R1
(E) NG

**3** This chart shows how many hours a family spent watching TV each week.

| Hours Watching TV | |
|---|---|
| Week 1 | 60 |
| Week 2 | 54 |
| Week 3 | 62 |
| Week 4 | 48 |
| Week 5 | 36 |

**What was the average number of hours spent watching TV per week?**

(A) 36 hours
(B) 48 hours
(C) 52 hours
(D) 260 hours
(E) NG

**4** A jumbo jet can carry 395 passengers.

**How many passengers can be carried on 4 of these jets?**

(A) 1185
(B) 1480
(C) 1560
(D) 1580
(E) NG

**5** $\frac{1}{5} + \frac{3}{10} =$

(A) $\frac{1}{2}$
(B) $\frac{2}{5}$
(C) $\frac{4}{15}$
(D) $\frac{7}{10}$
(E) NG

**6** 
$$\begin{array}{r} 6\frac{1}{4} \\ -\ \frac{3}{4} \\ \hline \end{array}$$

(A) 7
(B) $6\frac{1}{2}$
(C) $5\frac{1}{4}$
(D) $5\frac{1}{8}$
(E) NG

**GO ON** ⟹

# Practice Test 4 *(continued)*

**7** $\frac{1}{2} \times \frac{3}{8} =$

(A) $\frac{1}{4}$

(B) $\frac{3}{10}$

(C) $\frac{3}{16}$

(D) $\frac{2}{5}$

(E) NG

**8** Stan played the Duck Pond game at the fair. These colored ducks were in the Duck Pond.

| Color | Number of Ducks |
|-------|-----------------|
| Yellow | 20 |
| White | 15 |
| Red | 7 |
| Blue | 18 |

If Stan reaches in and takes out one duck without looking, what is the probability that the duck will be white?

(A) $\frac{1}{3}$

(B) $\frac{1}{4}$

(C) $\frac{1}{5}$

(D) $\frac{1}{6}$

(E) NG

**9** $\begin{array}{r} \$158.95 \\ + \quad 42.70 \\ \hline \end{array}$

(A) $191.25

(B) $191.65

(C) $200.65

(D) $201.65

(E) NG

**10** $\begin{array}{r} 80.91 \\ - \ 26.30 \\ \hline \end{array}$

(A) 107.21

(B) 66.61

(C) 64.61

(D) 52.61

(E) NG

**11** $8 \times 0.6 =$

(A) 0.48

(B) 4.8

(C) 48

(D) 480

(E) NG

**12** $4\overline{)28.12}$

(A) 6.03

(B) 6.93

(C) 7.03

(D) 7.3

(E) NG

**13** $\frac{2}{3} + \frac{5}{9} =$

(A) $\frac{7}{9}$

(B) $\frac{7}{12}$

(C) $1\frac{1}{9}$

(D) $1\frac{2}{9}$

(E) NG

**GO ON** →

# Practice Test 4 *(continued)*

**Use the graph below to answer questions 14 and 15.**

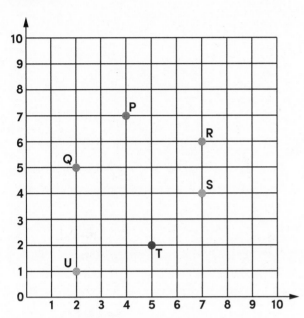

**14** **Where is point T located?**

Ⓐ (5, 2)

Ⓑ (2, 1)

Ⓒ (4, 7)

Ⓓ (2, 5)

Ⓔ NG

**15** **What point is located at (7, 4)?**

Ⓐ point P

Ⓑ point Q

Ⓒ point R

Ⓓ point S

Ⓔ NG

**16** 8% of 50 =

Ⓐ 2

Ⓑ 4

Ⓒ 8

Ⓓ 40

Ⓔ NG

**17** 30 is what percent of 40?

Ⓐ 30%

Ⓑ 50%

Ⓒ 60%

Ⓓ 75%

Ⓔ NG

**18** −12 + 9 =

Ⓐ −3

Ⓑ 3

Ⓒ −9

Ⓓ 21

Ⓔ NG

**19** 70% of $90 =

Ⓐ 20

Ⓑ 56

Ⓒ 65

Ⓓ 70

Ⓔ NG

**GO ON** ⇨

# Practice Test 4 (continued)

**20** This table shows the number of children who went to a summer camp each year.

| Children at Camp Wahoo | |
|---|---|
| Year | Number of Children |
| 2016 | 250 |
| 2017 | 320 |
| 2018 | 300 |
| 2019 | 370 |

What was the average number of children who went to the camp each year?

- (A) 310
- (B) 320
- (C) 360
- (D) 1240
- (E) NG

**21** If $3x - 2 = 10$, what is the value of $x$?

- (A) 4
- (B) 6
- (C) 8
- (D) 12
- (E) NG

**22** If $5n + 5 = 60$, what is the value of $n$?

- (A) 7
- (B) 9
- (C) 10
- (D) 11
- (E) NG

**23** If $7y > 21$, what is the value of $y$?

- (A) $y < 3$
- (B) $y < 2$
- (C) $y > 3$
- (D) $y > 2$
- (E) NG

**24** At 6:00 A.M., the temperature was 50°F. This table shows how much the temperature changed during the day.

| Time | Change in Temperature (°F) |
|---|---|
| 8:00 A.M. | +4 |
| 12:00 P.M. | −2 |
| 4:00 P.M. | −10 |
| 8:00 P.M. | +3 |

What was the temperature at 8:00 P.M.?

- (A) 39°F
- (B) 42°F
- (C) 45°F
- (D) 69°F
- (E) NG

**25** A shark gained $2\frac{1}{2}$ pounds per day. How much weight did the shark gain in 8 days?

- (A) $10\frac{1}{2}$ lb
- (B) 15 lb
- (C) $17\frac{1}{2}$ lb
- (D) 20 lb
- (E) NG

**STOP**

# Answer Sheet

Student Name _____   Grade _____

Teacher Name _____   Date _____

## MATHEMATICS

| | | |
|---|---|---|
| 1 Ⓐ Ⓑ Ⓒ Ⓓ Ⓔ | 11 Ⓐ Ⓑ Ⓒ Ⓓ Ⓔ | 21 Ⓐ Ⓑ Ⓒ Ⓓ Ⓔ |
| 2 Ⓐ Ⓑ Ⓒ Ⓓ Ⓔ | 12 Ⓐ Ⓑ Ⓒ Ⓓ Ⓔ | 22 Ⓐ Ⓑ Ⓒ Ⓓ Ⓔ |
| 3 Ⓐ Ⓑ Ⓒ Ⓓ Ⓔ | 13 Ⓐ Ⓑ Ⓒ Ⓓ Ⓔ | 23 Ⓐ Ⓑ Ⓒ Ⓓ Ⓔ |
| 4 Ⓐ Ⓑ Ⓒ Ⓓ Ⓔ | 14 Ⓐ Ⓑ Ⓒ Ⓓ Ⓔ | 24 Ⓐ Ⓑ Ⓒ Ⓓ Ⓔ |
| 5 Ⓐ Ⓑ Ⓒ Ⓓ Ⓔ | 15 Ⓐ Ⓑ Ⓒ Ⓓ Ⓔ | 25 Ⓐ Ⓑ Ⓒ Ⓓ Ⓔ |
| 6 Ⓐ Ⓑ Ⓒ Ⓓ Ⓔ | 16 Ⓐ Ⓑ Ⓒ Ⓓ Ⓔ | 26 Ⓐ Ⓑ Ⓒ Ⓓ Ⓔ |
| 7 Ⓐ Ⓑ Ⓒ Ⓓ Ⓔ | 17 Ⓐ Ⓑ Ⓒ Ⓓ Ⓔ | 27 Ⓐ Ⓑ Ⓒ Ⓓ Ⓔ |
| 8 Ⓐ Ⓑ Ⓒ Ⓓ Ⓔ | 18 Ⓐ Ⓑ Ⓒ Ⓓ Ⓔ | 28 Ⓐ Ⓑ Ⓒ Ⓓ Ⓔ |
| 9 Ⓐ Ⓑ Ⓒ Ⓓ Ⓔ | 19 Ⓐ Ⓑ Ⓒ Ⓓ Ⓔ | 29 Ⓐ Ⓑ Ⓒ Ⓓ Ⓔ |
| 10 Ⓐ Ⓑ Ⓒ Ⓓ Ⓔ | 20 Ⓐ Ⓑ Ⓒ Ⓓ Ⓔ | 30 Ⓐ Ⓑ Ⓒ Ⓓ Ⓔ |

# Practice Test 5: Numeration and Number Concepts

**Directions. Choose the best answer to each question. Mark your answer.**

**1** The population of a major U.S. city was 1,007,306. How should this number be written in words?

Ⓐ one billion seven million three hundred six

Ⓑ one million seven hundred thousand thirty-six

Ⓒ one million seven thousand three hundred six

Ⓓ one million seven thousand three hundred sixty

**2** A total of five million three hundred seventy thousand fifteen people visited a famous monument in one year. How should that be written in numerals?

Ⓐ 5,370,015

Ⓑ 5,307,015

Ⓒ 5,370,150

Ⓓ 5,037,015

**3** Which fraction is another name for $2\frac{1}{4}$?

Ⓐ $\frac{9}{4}$

Ⓑ $\frac{3}{4}$

Ⓒ $\frac{7}{4}$

Ⓓ $\frac{8}{4}$

**4** The chart shows the leading money winners in men's golf from 2016 to 2019.

| Year | Player | Earnings |
|------|--------|----------|
| 2019 | Brooks Koepka | $9,684,006 |
| 2018 | Justin Thomas | $8,694,821 |
| 2017 | Jordan Spieth | $9,153,033 |
| 2016 | Dustin Johnson | $9,067,685 |

Which list shows the players in order from least money to most money earned?

Ⓐ Thomas, Johnson, Spieth, Koepka

Ⓑ Spieth, Koepka, Thomas, Johnson

Ⓒ Koepka, Thomas, Spieth, Johnson

Ⓓ Johnson, Thomas, Koepka, Spieth

**5** Four white mice were weighed for a science experiment. Which mouse weighed least?

Ⓐ Mouse A: $1\frac{1}{4}$ ounces

Ⓑ Mouse B: $1\frac{1}{3}$ ounces

Ⓒ Mouse C: $1\frac{1}{5}$ ounces

Ⓓ Mouse D: $1\frac{1}{2}$ ounces

**GO ON** ➡

# Practice Test 5 *(continued)*

**6** This chart shows the average temperature on four planets.

| Planet | Average Temperature |
|--------|---------------------|
| Mercury | 332°F |
| Venus | 67°F |
| Mars | −82°F |
| Jupiter | −163°F |

Which planet has the lowest average temperature?

(A) Mercury

(B) Venus

(C) Mars

(D) Jupiter

**7** The Fabulous Pencil Company sold 37,992 pencils in 2021. What is that number rounded to the nearest ten thousand?

(A) 30,000

(B) 37,000

(C) 38,000

(D) 40,000

**8** There are about 1,380,004,385 people in India. What place value is represented by the 8 in 1,380,004,385?

(A) ten millions

(B) hundred millions

(C) millions

(D) billions

**9** 6,000,000 + 500,000 + 1000 + 70 =

(A) 6,501,070

(B) 6,051,070

(C) 6,005,170

(D) 6,510,70

**10** $4^5$ =

(A) $4 \times 4 \times 5$

(B) $4 \times 4 \times 4 \times 4 \times 4$

(C) $4 \times 5 \times 4 \times 5$

(D) $4 + 4 + 4 + 4 + 4$

**11** Charlotte created this number pattern.

2, 6, 18, 54, _____

If this pattern continues, what number should come next?

(A) 55

(B) 108

(C) 152

(D) 162

**12** $\frac{65}{100}$ =

(A) 0.065

(B) 0.65

(C) 6.5

(D) 65

GO ON

## Practice Test 5 *(continued)*

**13** Louis made this pattern with tiles.

Which square fits in the empty space to complete the pattern?

(A)

(C)

(B)

(D)

**14** Which numbers are both factors of 45?

(A) 4, 11

(B) 5, 9

(C) 6, 7

(D) 8, 10

**15** What is the least common multiple of 3, 6, and 10?

(A) 60

(B) 30

(C) 18

(D) 10

**16** The Sterling Train Line has been running for three months. In the first month, 18,370 passengers rode the train. There were 22,095 passengers in the second month and 26,810 passengers in the third month. About how many passengers in all rode the train in those three months?

(A) 48,000

(B) 67,000

(C) 75,000

(D) 90,000

**17** In 2020, the population of Idaho was 1,839,106. The population of Maine was 1,362,359. About how many more people lived in Idaho than in Maine?

(A) 30,000

(B) 200,000

(C) 300,000

(D) 400,000

**18** Look at the number line.

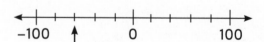

The arrow is pointing to what number on the number line?

(A) 60

(B) 80

(C) –30

(D) –60

**GO ON**

# Practice Test 5 *(continued)*

**19** What fractional part of the figure is shaded?

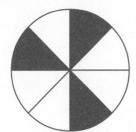

Ⓐ $\frac{3}{8}$

Ⓑ $\frac{1}{3}$

Ⓒ $\frac{3}{5}$

Ⓓ $\frac{5}{8}$

**20** Of the 160 students in a school, 32 have red hair. What fractional part of the students have red hair?

Ⓐ $\frac{1}{5}$

Ⓑ $\frac{1}{3}$

Ⓒ $\frac{1}{4}$

Ⓓ $\frac{1}{6}$

**21** Which number sentence is true?

Ⓐ $3\frac{1}{2} \times 0 = 3\frac{1}{2}$

Ⓑ $\frac{9}{5} \times 1 = 1$

Ⓒ $\frac{1}{7} + \frac{6}{7} = 7$

Ⓓ $\frac{1}{3} \times \frac{2}{7} = \frac{2}{7} \times \frac{1}{3}$

**22** This chart shows the average price of concert tickets for different bands in 2019.

| Performer | Average Ticket Price |
|---|---|
| Band A | $56.61 |
| Band B | $57.37 |
| Band C | $53.92 |
| Band D | $55.02 |

Which band had the highest average ticket price?

Ⓐ Band A

Ⓑ Band B

Ⓒ Band C

Ⓓ Band D

**23** Look at the number line.

The arrow is pointing to what number on the number line?

Ⓐ $1\frac{1}{2}$

Ⓑ $1\frac{1}{4}$

Ⓒ $1\frac{2}{5}$

Ⓓ $1\frac{2}{3}$

**STOP**

# Answer Sheet

Student Name _____  Grade _____

Teacher Name _____  Date _____

## MATHEMATICS

| | | |
|---|---|---|
| 1 Ⓐ Ⓑ Ⓒ Ⓓ Ⓔ | 11 Ⓐ Ⓑ Ⓒ Ⓓ Ⓔ | 21 Ⓐ Ⓑ Ⓒ Ⓓ Ⓔ |
| 2 Ⓐ Ⓑ Ⓒ Ⓓ Ⓔ | 12 Ⓐ Ⓑ Ⓒ Ⓓ Ⓔ | 22 Ⓐ Ⓑ Ⓒ Ⓓ Ⓔ |
| 3 Ⓐ Ⓑ Ⓒ Ⓓ Ⓔ | 13 Ⓐ Ⓑ Ⓒ Ⓓ Ⓔ | 23 Ⓐ Ⓑ Ⓒ Ⓓ Ⓔ |
| 4 Ⓐ Ⓑ Ⓒ Ⓓ Ⓔ | 14 Ⓐ Ⓑ Ⓒ Ⓓ Ⓔ | 24 Ⓐ Ⓑ Ⓒ Ⓓ Ⓔ |
| 5 Ⓐ Ⓑ Ⓒ Ⓓ Ⓔ | 15 Ⓐ Ⓑ Ⓒ Ⓓ Ⓔ | 25 Ⓐ Ⓑ Ⓒ Ⓓ Ⓔ |
| 6 Ⓐ Ⓑ Ⓒ Ⓓ Ⓔ | 16 Ⓐ Ⓑ Ⓒ Ⓓ Ⓔ | 26 Ⓐ Ⓑ Ⓒ Ⓓ Ⓔ |
| 7 Ⓐ Ⓑ Ⓒ Ⓓ Ⓔ | 17 Ⓐ Ⓑ Ⓒ Ⓓ Ⓔ | 27 Ⓐ Ⓑ Ⓒ Ⓓ Ⓔ |
| 8 Ⓐ Ⓑ Ⓒ Ⓓ Ⓔ | 18 Ⓐ Ⓑ Ⓒ Ⓓ Ⓔ | 28 Ⓐ Ⓑ Ⓒ Ⓓ Ⓔ |
| 9 Ⓐ Ⓑ Ⓒ Ⓓ Ⓔ | 19 Ⓐ Ⓑ Ⓒ Ⓓ Ⓔ | 29 Ⓐ Ⓑ Ⓒ Ⓓ Ⓔ |
| 10 Ⓐ Ⓑ Ⓒ Ⓓ Ⓔ | 20 Ⓐ Ⓑ Ⓒ Ⓓ Ⓔ | 30 Ⓐ Ⓑ Ⓒ Ⓓ Ⓔ |

Name _____  Date _____

## Practice Test 6: Geometry and Measurement

**Directions.** Choose the best answer to each question. Mark your answer.

**1** Which figure has 3 faces?

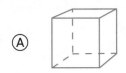 Ⓐ

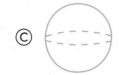 Ⓒ

Ⓑ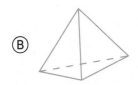

Ⓓ

**2** A soccer field is 120 yards long. How many feet is that?

Ⓐ 360
Ⓑ 240
Ⓒ 60
Ⓓ 40

**3** What is the perimeter of this figure? Use a centimeter ruler.

Ⓐ 10 cm
Ⓑ 18 cm
Ⓒ 20 cm
Ⓓ 24 cm

**4** Which figure has no parallel sides?

Ⓐ

Ⓒ

Ⓑ

Ⓓ

**5** Which figure is congruent to Figure A?

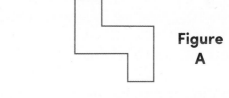

**Figure A**

Ⓐ

Ⓒ

Ⓑ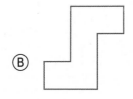

Ⓓ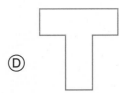

**6** Which name has a line of symmetry?

Ⓐ DA|VE    Ⓒ TORI

Ⓑ OT|TO    Ⓓ CHER

 **GO ON**

# Practice Test 6 *(continued)*

**7** Mrs. Eames bought a bag of apples with a mass of 4.2 kilograms. How many grams is that?

Ⓐ 4200

Ⓑ 420

Ⓒ 42

Ⓓ 0.42

**8** Which unit should be used to measure the amount of milk in a paper cup?

Ⓐ pints

Ⓑ gallons

Ⓒ ounces

Ⓓ quarts

**9** This diagram shows the new deck that Mr. Cohn plans to build.

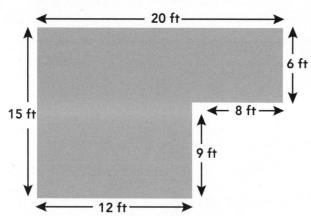

What is the area of the deck?

Ⓐ 70 sq ft

Ⓑ 160 sq ft

Ⓒ 180 sq ft

Ⓓ 228 sq ft

**10** The Big Top circus gave 3 shows. There were 1890 people at the first show, 2015 people at the second show, and 2970 people at the third show. <u>About</u> how many people in all went to the circus?

Ⓐ 3000

Ⓑ 5000

Ⓒ 7000

Ⓓ 10,000

**11** A clay tile weighs $10\frac{1}{4}$ ounces. <u>About</u> how many ounces do 97 tiles weigh?

Ⓐ 100 oz

Ⓑ 500 oz

Ⓒ 1000 oz

Ⓓ 1500 oz

**12** Which figure is a trapezoid?

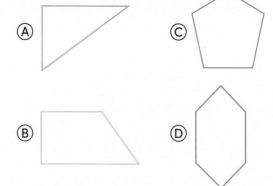

GO ON

# Practice Test 6 *(continued)*

The graph below shows the top five producers of maple syrup in 2020. Use the graph to answer questions 13 and 14.

**Top Maple Syrup Producers: 2020**

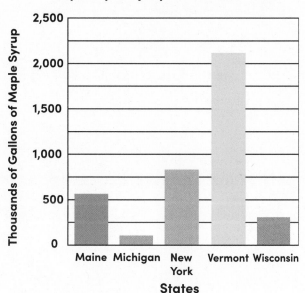

**13** Which state produced the most maple syrup?

Ⓐ Maine

Ⓑ New York

Ⓒ Wisconsin

Ⓓ Vermont

**14** **About** how much maple syrup did Wisconsin produce?

Ⓐ 150,000 gal

Ⓑ 250,000 gal

Ⓒ 300,000 gal

Ⓓ 350,000 gal

**15** An adult man is most likely to have a mass of:

Ⓐ 100 milligrams

Ⓑ 100 grams

Ⓒ 100 kilograms

Ⓓ 100 tons

Use the figure below to answer questions 16 and 17.

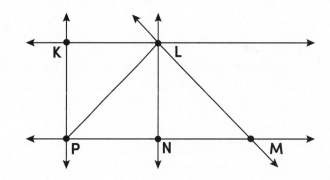

**16** Which angle is less than 90 degrees?

Ⓐ ∠MLN

Ⓑ ∠KPN

Ⓒ ∠KLM

Ⓓ ∠LNP

**17** Which is parallel to $\overline{KP}$?

Ⓐ $\overline{PL}$

Ⓑ $\overline{LN}$

Ⓒ $\overline{PM}$

Ⓓ $\overline{LM}$

**GO ON**

# Practice Test 6 *(continued)*

Use this map and an inch ruler to answer questions 18 and 19.

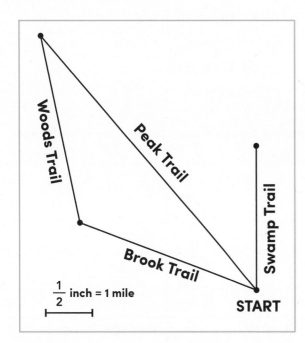

18. **What is the actual distance from the START to the end of the Swamp Trail?**

    Ⓐ $\frac{3}{4}$ miles          Ⓒ 2 miles

    Ⓑ $1\frac{1}{2}$ miles          Ⓓ 3 miles

19. **Jed hiked from the START to the end of the Peak Trail. Then he hiked back on the Woods Trail and the Brook Trail. How far did he hike in all?**

    Ⓐ 15 miles          Ⓒ 9 miles

    Ⓑ 12 miles          Ⓓ $7\frac{1}{2}$ miles

20. **This figure will be turned 180° in the direction shown.**

**What will the figure look like after it has been turned?**

Ⓐ
Ⓒ

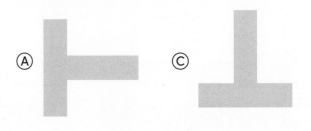

Ⓑ
Ⓓ

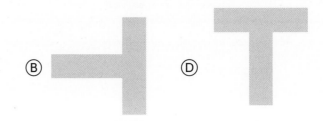

STOP

# Answer Sheet

Student Name _____ Grade _____

Teacher Name _____ Date _____

## MATHEMATICS

| 1 | Ⓐ Ⓑ Ⓒ Ⓓ Ⓔ | 11 | Ⓐ Ⓑ Ⓒ Ⓓ Ⓔ | 21 | Ⓐ Ⓑ Ⓒ Ⓓ Ⓔ |
|---|---|---|---|---|---|
| 2 | Ⓐ Ⓑ Ⓒ Ⓓ Ⓔ | 12 | Ⓐ Ⓑ Ⓒ Ⓓ Ⓔ | 22 | Ⓐ Ⓑ Ⓒ Ⓓ Ⓔ |
| 3 | Ⓐ Ⓑ Ⓒ Ⓓ Ⓔ | 13 | Ⓐ Ⓑ Ⓒ Ⓓ Ⓔ | 23 | Ⓐ Ⓑ Ⓒ Ⓓ Ⓔ |
| 4 | Ⓐ Ⓑ Ⓒ Ⓓ Ⓔ | 14 | Ⓐ Ⓑ Ⓒ Ⓓ Ⓔ | 24 | Ⓐ Ⓑ Ⓒ Ⓓ Ⓔ |
| 5 | Ⓐ Ⓑ Ⓒ Ⓓ Ⓔ | 15 | Ⓐ Ⓑ Ⓒ Ⓓ Ⓔ | 25 | Ⓐ Ⓑ Ⓒ Ⓓ Ⓔ |
| 6 | Ⓐ Ⓑ Ⓒ Ⓓ Ⓔ | 16 | Ⓐ Ⓑ Ⓒ Ⓓ Ⓔ | 26 | Ⓐ Ⓑ Ⓒ Ⓓ Ⓔ |
| 7 | Ⓐ Ⓑ Ⓒ Ⓓ Ⓔ | 17 | Ⓐ Ⓑ Ⓒ Ⓓ Ⓔ | 27 | Ⓐ Ⓑ Ⓒ Ⓓ Ⓔ |
| 8 | Ⓐ Ⓑ Ⓒ Ⓓ Ⓔ | 18 | Ⓐ Ⓑ Ⓒ Ⓓ Ⓔ | 28 | Ⓐ Ⓑ Ⓒ Ⓓ Ⓔ |
| 9 | Ⓐ Ⓑ Ⓒ Ⓓ Ⓔ | 19 | Ⓐ Ⓑ Ⓒ Ⓓ Ⓔ | 29 | Ⓐ Ⓑ Ⓒ Ⓓ Ⓔ |
| 10 | Ⓐ Ⓑ Ⓒ Ⓓ Ⓔ | 20 | Ⓐ Ⓑ Ⓒ Ⓓ Ⓔ | 30 | Ⓐ Ⓑ Ⓒ Ⓓ Ⓔ |

# Practice Test 7: Problem Solving

**Directions.** Choose the best answer to each question. Mark your answer. If the correct answer is *not given*, choose "NG."

**1** In an airplane, there are 32 rows of seats and 6 seats in each row. How many seats are there in all?

Ⓐ 38
Ⓑ 182
Ⓒ 192
Ⓓ 202
Ⓔ NG

**2** Collin bought these 3 albums.

$24.95     $16.90     $14.75

What is the total cost of these albums?

Ⓐ $56.60
Ⓑ $54.60
Ⓒ $41.85
Ⓓ $39.70
Ⓔ NG

**3** Sela jogged $2\frac{1}{2}$ miles to the lake. Then she jogged $3\frac{3}{4}$ miles on the way back. How far did she jog in all?

Ⓐ $5\frac{1}{4}$ miles
Ⓑ $5\frac{1}{2}$ miles
Ⓒ 6 miles
Ⓓ $6\frac{1}{2}$ miles
Ⓔ NG

**4** A total of 160 children play in the city soccer league, and 64 of the players are girls. What percent of the players are girls?

Ⓐ 96%
Ⓑ 56%
Ⓒ 40%
Ⓓ 30%
Ⓔ NG

**5** Boxes of greeting cards cost $7.95 each, or you can buy a set of 3 boxes for $20.00.

$7.95        $20.00

How much do you save on 3 boxes if you buy the set?

Ⓐ $23.85
Ⓑ $3.85
Ⓒ $2.95
Ⓓ $1.75
Ⓔ NG

**GO ON**

# Practice Test 7 *(continued)*

**6** Caroline wants to buy a scooter that usually costs $105.00. The scooter is on sale.

What is the sale price of the scooter?

Ⓐ $40.00

Ⓑ $42.00

Ⓒ $53.00

Ⓓ $63.00

Ⓔ NG

**7** Jackson started writing a story at 8:30 A.M. He stopped writing at 1:15 P.M. How long did he write?

Ⓐ 3 hr, 45 min

Ⓑ 3 hr, 55 min

Ⓒ 4 hr, 15 min

Ⓓ 4 hr, 30 min

Ⓔ NG

**8** A paperback book costs $8.95. <u>About</u> how much would 58 of these books cost?

Ⓐ $400          Ⓒ $480

Ⓑ $450          Ⓓ $540

**9** At the car wash, 6 cars are washed every 15 minutes. At this rate, how long would it take to wash 24 cars?

Ⓐ 1 hour

Ⓑ 50 min

Ⓒ 40 min

Ⓓ 36 min

Ⓔ NG

**10** Five students stood in line for lunch in the cafeteria. Mandy stood in front of John and behind Gary. Fran stood in front of Gary and behind Claude. Who was first in line?

Ⓐ Claude

Ⓑ Fran

Ⓒ Mandy

Ⓓ John

Ⓔ NG

**11** A mason can lay 20 bricks in 30 minutes. At this rate, how long will it take him to lay 100 bricks?

Ⓐ 60 minutes

Ⓑ 90 minutes

Ⓒ 120 minutes

Ⓓ 150 minutes

Ⓔ NG

GO ON

# Practice Test 7 *(continued)*

**12** Mrs. Charles rides 12 miles a day on her bike. <u>About</u> how many miles will she ride in 29 days?

Ⓐ 300

Ⓑ 500

Ⓒ 700

Ⓓ 900

**13** For 5 days, Stacey waited on customers at the pet store. She waited on 31 customers on the first day and 40 customers on the second day. What else do you need to know to find the average number of customers she waited on each day?

Ⓐ the total number of customers in the 5 days

Ⓑ how many customers she served on the last day

Ⓒ on which days of the week she worked

Ⓓ the number of pets she sold in those 5 days

**14** On average, 118 cars go through the toll booth each hour. How many cars go through the toll booth in 8 hours?

Ⓐ 126

Ⓑ 864

Ⓒ 934

Ⓓ 1044

Ⓔ NG

**15** Garrett mows lawns for $10 an hour. Last week he earned $140 mowing lawns. Which question can you answer from this information?

Ⓐ How many lawns did Garrett mow?

Ⓑ What is the average amount of money Garrett earns each week?

Ⓒ How many hours did Garrett spend mowing lawns last week?

Ⓓ How much money does Garrett make during the summer?

Ⓔ NG

**16** A store owner received 18 cases of soda. Each case has 24 cans of soda. The owner sells each can for $0.60. Which number sentence should you use to find how much money the owner will collect if he sells all the soda?

Ⓐ (18 × 24) + $0.60 = ☐

Ⓑ (18 × 24) × $0.60 = ☐

Ⓒ (18 × 24) ÷ $0.60 = ☐

Ⓓ (18 × 24) − $0.60 = ☐

Ⓔ NG

**GO ON** →

# Practice Test 7 *(continued)*

**17** Mr. Clemens and his daughter caught 30 fish one day. Of those fish, 18 were flounder. What percent of the fish were flounder?

- Ⓐ 30%
- Ⓑ 40%
- Ⓒ 50%
- Ⓓ 70%
- Ⓔ NG

**18** Janine was making potato salad for a picnic. She used $8\frac{3}{4}$ pounds of russet potatoes and $6\frac{5}{8}$ pounds of Idaho potatoes.

$8\frac{3}{4}$ lb          $6\frac{5}{8}$ lb

How many pounds of potatoes did she use in all?

- Ⓐ $14\frac{1}{8}$ lb
- Ⓑ $14\frac{3}{8}$ lb
- Ⓒ $15\frac{1}{8}$ lb
- Ⓓ $15\frac{3}{8}$ lb
- Ⓔ NG

**19** Ms. Lopis bought 2 pairs of skis at a ski sale.

SKI SALE
$390/PAIR

Including a sales tax of 6%, what was the total cost of the 2 pairs of skis?

- Ⓐ $826.80
- Ⓑ $790.00
- Ⓒ $413.40
- Ⓓ $390.00
- Ⓔ NG

**20** At the movie theater, 102 adults and 60 children went to the discount show. Adults paid $6.50 per ticket. Children's tickets were $4.00 each.

ADMIT ONE $6.50          ADMIT ONE $4.00

How much money was spent on tickets?

- Ⓐ $903.00
- Ⓑ $863.00
- Ⓒ $663.00
- Ⓓ $240.00
- Ⓔ NG

STOP

# Answer Sheet

# Practice Test 7

Student Name _____

Grade _____

Teacher Name _____

Date _____

## MATHEMATICS

| | | |
|---|---|---|
| 1 Ⓐ Ⓑ Ⓒ Ⓓ Ⓔ | 11 Ⓐ Ⓑ Ⓒ Ⓓ Ⓔ | 21 Ⓐ Ⓑ Ⓒ Ⓓ Ⓔ |
| 2 Ⓐ Ⓑ Ⓒ Ⓓ Ⓔ | 12 Ⓐ Ⓑ Ⓒ Ⓓ Ⓔ | 22 Ⓐ Ⓑ Ⓒ Ⓓ Ⓔ |
| 3 Ⓐ Ⓑ Ⓒ Ⓓ Ⓔ | 13 Ⓐ Ⓑ Ⓒ Ⓓ Ⓔ | 23 Ⓐ Ⓑ Ⓒ Ⓓ Ⓔ |
| 4 Ⓐ Ⓑ Ⓒ Ⓓ Ⓔ | 14 Ⓐ Ⓑ Ⓒ Ⓓ Ⓔ | 24 Ⓐ Ⓑ Ⓒ Ⓓ Ⓔ |
| 5 Ⓐ Ⓑ Ⓒ Ⓓ Ⓔ | 15 Ⓐ Ⓑ Ⓒ Ⓓ Ⓔ | 25 Ⓐ Ⓑ Ⓒ Ⓓ Ⓔ |
| 6 Ⓐ Ⓑ Ⓒ Ⓓ Ⓔ | 16 Ⓐ Ⓑ Ⓒ Ⓓ Ⓔ | 26 Ⓐ Ⓑ Ⓒ Ⓓ Ⓔ |
| 7 Ⓐ Ⓑ Ⓒ Ⓓ Ⓔ | 17 Ⓐ Ⓑ Ⓒ Ⓓ Ⓔ | 27 Ⓐ Ⓑ Ⓒ Ⓓ Ⓔ |
| 8 Ⓐ Ⓑ Ⓒ Ⓓ Ⓔ | 18 Ⓐ Ⓑ Ⓒ Ⓓ Ⓔ | 28 Ⓐ Ⓑ Ⓒ Ⓓ Ⓔ |
| 9 Ⓐ Ⓑ Ⓒ Ⓓ Ⓔ | 19 Ⓐ Ⓑ Ⓒ Ⓓ Ⓔ | 29 Ⓐ Ⓑ Ⓒ Ⓓ Ⓔ |
| 10 Ⓐ Ⓑ Ⓒ Ⓓ Ⓔ | 20 Ⓐ Ⓑ Ⓒ Ⓓ Ⓔ | 30 Ⓐ Ⓑ Ⓒ Ⓓ Ⓔ |

# Practice Test 8: Computation

**Directions.** Choose the best answer to each question. Mark your answer.
If the correct answer is *not given*, choose "NG."

**1**
$$\begin{array}{r} 65 \\ \times\ 28 \end{array}$$

  Ⓐ 650
  Ⓑ 1820
  Ⓒ 1828
  Ⓓ 1920
  Ⓔ NG

**2** $35\overline{)490}$

  Ⓐ 14
  Ⓑ 15
  Ⓒ 16
  Ⓓ 17
  Ⓔ NG

**3** A passenger ferry can carry 462 passengers.

How many passengers can the ferry carry in 3 trips?

  Ⓐ 924
  Ⓑ 1396
  Ⓒ 1406
  Ⓓ 1848
  Ⓔ NG

**4** $\frac{1}{6} + \frac{5}{12} =$

  Ⓐ $\frac{6}{18}$
  Ⓑ $\frac{7}{12}$
  Ⓒ $\frac{1}{3}$
  Ⓓ $\frac{5}{7}$
  Ⓔ NG

**5**
$$\begin{array}{r} 4\frac{1}{3} \\ -\ \ \frac{2}{3} \end{array}$$

  Ⓐ $2\frac{2}{3}$
  Ⓑ 3
  Ⓒ $3\frac{1}{3}$
  Ⓓ 4
  Ⓔ NG

**6** $\frac{1}{4} \times \frac{4}{5} =$

  Ⓐ $\frac{3}{20}$
  Ⓑ $\frac{4}{9}$
  Ⓒ $\frac{3}{10}$
  Ⓓ $\frac{1}{5}$
  Ⓔ NG

**7** $7\overline{)212}$

  Ⓐ 30
  Ⓑ 30 R1
  Ⓒ 30 R2
  Ⓓ 31 R2
  Ⓔ NG

**GO ON** ⟶

# Practice Test 8 *(continued)*

**8** Greg has 2 different bike helmets, 6 shirts, and 3 pairs of bike shorts.

| Biking Gear | | |
|---|---|---|
| Helmets | Shirts | Shorts |
| 2 | 6 | 3 |

How many different combinations of 1 helmet, 1 shirt, and 1 pair of shorts can he make?

(A) 11

(B) 24

(C) 36

(D) 48

(E) NG

**9** Melanie played a fishing game at the fair. These colored fish were in the fish tank.

| Color | Number of Fish |
|---|---|
| Red | 25 |
| Green | 30 |
| White | 25 |
| Blue | 20 |

If Melanie catches one fish without looking, what is the probability that the fish will be blue?

(A) $\frac{1}{3}$

(B) $\frac{1}{4}$

(C) $\frac{1}{5}$

(D) $\frac{1}{6}$

(E) NG

**10**
$$\begin{array}{r} \$148.25 \\ + \phantom{0}79.80 \end{array}$$

(A) $68.45

(B) $227.05

(C) $227.65

(D) $228.05

(E) NG

**11**
$$\begin{array}{r} 61.05 \\ - 38.29 \end{array}$$

(A) 99.34

(B) 37.26

(C) 22.76

(D) 21.86

(E) NG

**12** $4 \times 0.9 =$

(A) 360

(B) 36

(C) 3.6

(D) 0.36

(E) NG

**13** $6\overline{)48.3}$

(A) 8.5

(B) 8.05

(C) 7.5

(D) 7.05

(E) NG

**14** $\frac{3}{4} + \frac{3}{8} =$

(A) $\frac{1}{2}$

(B) $1\frac{1}{4}$

(C) $\frac{6}{12}$

(D) $1\frac{1}{8}$

(E) NG

GO ON

# Practice Test 8 *(continued)*

Use the graph below to answer questions 15 and 16.

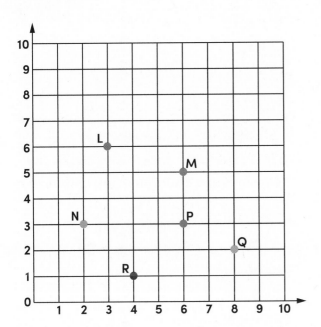

**15** Where is point Q located?

Ⓐ (4, 1)

Ⓑ (2, 8)

Ⓒ (3, 6)

Ⓓ (8, 2)

Ⓔ NG

**16** What point is located at (6, 5)?

Ⓐ point M

Ⓑ point N

Ⓒ point P

Ⓓ point R

Ⓔ NG

**17** 12% of 50 =

Ⓐ 5

Ⓑ 6

Ⓒ 38

Ⓓ 60

Ⓔ NG

**18** 80% of $60 =

Ⓐ $14

Ⓑ $30

Ⓒ $40

Ⓓ $42

Ⓔ NG

**19** 15 is what percent of 30?

Ⓐ 15%

Ⓑ 30%

Ⓒ 45%

Ⓓ 50%

Ⓔ NG

**20** −15 + 8 =

Ⓐ 23

Ⓑ −8

Ⓒ 7

Ⓓ −7

Ⓔ NG

**GO ON**

# Practice Test 8 *(continued)*

**21** This table lists the scores Merrill got on 5 spelling tests.

| Test | Score |
|------|-------|
| 1 | 65 |
| 2 | 90 |
| 3 | 84 |
| 4 | 78 |
| 5 | 82 |

What was Merrill's median test score?

Ⓐ 65
Ⓑ 78
Ⓒ 82
Ⓓ 84
Ⓔ NG

**22** If $5x - 4 = 31$, what is the value of $x$?

Ⓐ 6
Ⓑ 7
Ⓒ 8
Ⓓ 10
Ⓔ NG

**23** If $3n + 8 = 44$, what is the value of $n$?

Ⓐ 6
Ⓑ 8
Ⓒ 10
Ⓓ 12
Ⓔ NG

**24** If $6y > 24$, what is the value of $y$?

Ⓐ $y < 3$
Ⓑ $y < 4$
Ⓒ $y > 3$
Ⓓ $y > 4$
Ⓔ NG

**25** At 4:00 A.M., the temperature was 30°F. This table shows how much the temperature changed during the day.

| Day | Change in Temperature (°F) |
|------|-------|
| 10:00 A.M. | −6 |
| 2:00 P.M. | +4 |
| 6:00 P.M. | −2 |
| 10:00 P.M. | −5 |

What was the temperature at 10:00 P.M.?

Ⓐ 21°F
Ⓑ 32°F
Ⓒ 35°F
Ⓓ 47°F
Ⓔ NG

STOP

# Answer Sheet

Student Name _____   Grade _____

Teacher Name _____   Date _____

## MATHEMATICS

| 1 | Ⓐ Ⓑ Ⓒ Ⓓ Ⓔ | 11 | Ⓐ Ⓑ Ⓒ Ⓓ Ⓔ | 21 | Ⓐ Ⓑ Ⓒ Ⓓ Ⓔ |
|---|---|---|---|---|---|
| 2 | Ⓐ Ⓑ Ⓒ Ⓓ Ⓔ | 12 | Ⓐ Ⓑ Ⓒ Ⓓ Ⓔ | 22 | Ⓐ Ⓑ Ⓒ Ⓓ Ⓔ |
| 3 | Ⓐ Ⓑ Ⓒ Ⓓ Ⓔ | 13 | Ⓐ Ⓑ Ⓒ Ⓓ Ⓔ | 23 | Ⓐ Ⓑ Ⓒ Ⓓ Ⓔ |
| 4 | Ⓐ Ⓑ Ⓒ Ⓓ Ⓔ | 14 | Ⓐ Ⓑ Ⓒ Ⓓ Ⓔ | 24 | Ⓐ Ⓑ Ⓒ Ⓓ Ⓔ |
| 5 | Ⓐ Ⓑ Ⓒ Ⓓ Ⓔ | 15 | Ⓐ Ⓑ Ⓒ Ⓓ Ⓔ | 25 | Ⓐ Ⓑ Ⓒ Ⓓ Ⓔ |
| 6 | Ⓐ Ⓑ Ⓒ Ⓓ Ⓔ | 16 | Ⓐ Ⓑ Ⓒ Ⓓ Ⓔ | 26 | Ⓐ Ⓑ Ⓒ Ⓓ Ⓔ |
| 7 | Ⓐ Ⓑ Ⓒ Ⓓ Ⓔ | 17 | Ⓐ Ⓑ Ⓒ Ⓓ Ⓔ | 27 | Ⓐ Ⓑ Ⓒ Ⓓ Ⓔ |
| 8 | Ⓐ Ⓑ Ⓒ Ⓓ Ⓔ | 18 | Ⓐ Ⓑ Ⓒ Ⓓ Ⓔ | 28 | Ⓐ Ⓑ Ⓒ Ⓓ Ⓔ |
| 9 | Ⓐ Ⓑ Ⓒ Ⓓ Ⓔ | 19 | Ⓐ Ⓑ Ⓒ Ⓓ Ⓔ | 29 | Ⓐ Ⓑ Ⓒ Ⓓ Ⓔ |
| 10 | Ⓐ Ⓑ Ⓒ Ⓓ Ⓔ | 20 | Ⓐ Ⓑ Ⓒ Ⓓ Ⓔ | 30 | Ⓐ Ⓑ Ⓒ Ⓓ Ⓔ |

# TESTED SKILLS

## Practice Test 1: Numeration and Number Concepts

| Tested Skills | Item Numbers |
|---|---|
| Associate numerals and number words | 1, 2 |
| Compare and order whole numbers and integers | 4, 5, 6 |
| Use place value and rounding | 7, 9 |
| Use exponents and expanded forms | 3, 10, 11 |
| Identify patterns | 8, 12 |
| Identify prime numbers, factors, and multiples | 13, 14 |
| Estimation | 15, 16 |
| Use a number line | 17, 25 |
| Identify fractional parts | 18, 19 |
| Compare and order fractions and decimals | 20, 22 |
| Rename fractions, decimals, and percents | 23, 24 |
| Apply operational properties | 21 |

## Practice Test 2: Geometry and Measurement

| Tested Skills | Item Numbers |
|---|---|
| Identify parts and characteristics of plane and solid figures | 2, 11 |
| Recognize symmetry and congruence | 5, 6 |
| Identify points, lines, line segments, and angles | 4, 15, 16 |
| Identify transformations | 20 |
| Find perimeter, circumference, area, and volume | 3, 19 |
| Use appropriate units of measurement | 8, 14 |
| Convert units of measure (standard, metric) | 1, 7 |
| Estimate measurements | 9, 10 |
| Use scale to determine distance | 17, 18 |
| Interpret graphs, charts, and tables | 12, 13 |

## Practice Test 3: Problem Solving

| Tested Skills | Item Numbers |
|---|---|
| Solve problems involving basic operations | 1, 8, 9, 15 |
| Solve problems involving money, time, and measurement | 2, 6 |
| Solve problems involving percents and discount | 3, 5, 16 |
| Use estimation to solve problems | 11, 12, 13 |
| Solve problems involving ratio, proportion, and logic | 7, 10 |
| Identify steps in solving problems | 14 |
| Solve multi-step problems | 4, 17, 18 |

## Practice Test 4: Computation

| Tested Skills | Item Numbers |
|---|---|
| Compute with whole numbers | 1, 2, 4 |
| Compute with fractions and mixed numbers | 5, 6, 7, 13, 25 |
| Compute with decimals | 9, 10, 11, 12 |
| Find percents | 16, 17, 19 |
| Complete operations with integers | 18, 24 |
| Find average, median, probability, and combinations | 3, 8, 20 |
| Solve simple equations and inequalities | 21, 22, 23 |
| Find/plot points on a coordinate graph | 14, 15 |

## Practice Test 5: Numeration and Number Concepts

| Tested Skills | Item Numbers |
|---|---|
| Associate numerals and number words | 1, 2 |
| Compare and order whole numbers and integers | 4, 6 |
| Use place value and rounding | 7, 8 |
| Use exponents and expanded forms | 9, 10 |
| Identify patterns | 11, 13 |
| Identify prime numbers, factors, and multiples | 14, 15 |
| Estimation | 16, 17 |
| Use a number line | 18, 23 |
| Identify fractional parts | 19, 20 |
| Compare and order fractions and decimals | 5, 22 |
| Rename fractions, decimals, and percents | 3, 12 |
| Apply operational properties | 21 |

## Practice Test 6: Geometry and Measurement

| Tested Skills | Item Numbers |
|---|---|
| Identify parts and characteristics of plane and solid figures | 1, 4, 12 |
| Recognize symmetry and congruence | 5, 6 |
| Identify points, lines, line segments, and angles | 16, 17 |
| Identify transformations | 20 |
| Find perimeter, circumference, area, and volume | 3, 9 |
| Use appropriate units of measurement | 8, 15 |
| Convert units of measure (standard, metric) | 2, 7 |
| Estimate measurements | 10, 11 |
| Use scale to determine distance | 18, 19 |
| Interpret graphs, charts, and tables | 13, 14 |

## Practice Test 7: Problem Solving

| Tested Skills | Item Numbers |
|---|---|
| Solve problems involving basic operations | 1, 3, 14 |
| Solve problems involving money, time, and measurement | 2, 7, 18 |
| Solve problems involving percents and discount | 4, 6, 17 |
| Use estimation to solve problems | 8, 12 |
| Solve problems involving ratio, proportion, and logic | 9, 10, 11 |
| Identify steps in solving problems | 13, 15, 16 |
| Solve multi-step problems | 5, 19, 20 |

## Practice Test 8: Computation

| Tested Skills | Item Numbers |
|---|---|
| Compute with whole numbers | 1, 2, 3, 7 |
| Compute with fractions and mixed numbers | 4, 5, 6, 14 |
| Compute with decimals | 10, 11, 12, 13 |
| Find percents | 17, 18, 19 |
| Complete operations with integers | 20, 25 |
| Find average, median, probability, and combinations | 8, 9, 21 |
| Solve simple equations and inequalities | 22, 23, 24 |
| Find/plot points on a coordinate graph | 15, 16 |

# ANSWER KEYS

## Practice Test 1
**Numeration and Number Concepts**

1. B
2. C
3. D
4. A
5. A
6. B
7. A
8. C
9. C
10. C
11. B
12. C
13. D
14. B
15. C
16. A
17. B
18. B
19. A
20. D
21. B
22. D
23. A
24. C
25. C

## Practice Test 2
**Geometry and Measurement**

1. B
2. A
3. D
4. A
5. B
6. B
7. D
8. C
9. C
10. B
11. C
12. D
13. D
14. A
15. D
16. B
17. B
18. D
19. A
20. C

## Practice Test 3
**Problem Solving**

1. B
2. D
3. B
4. A
5. C
6. E
7. D
8. C
9. C
10. D
11. C
12. C
13. B
14. D
15. B
16. E
17. E
18. A

## Practice Test 4
**Computation**

1. C
2. E
3. C
4. D
5. A
6. E
7. C
8. B
9. D
10. E
11. B
12. C
13. D
14. A
15. D
16. B
17. D
18. A
19. E
20. A
21. A
22. D
23. C
24. C
25. D

## Practice Test 5
**Numeration and Number Concepts**

1. C
2. A
3. A
4. A
5. C
6. D
7. D
8. A
9. A
10. B
11. D
12. B
13. C
14. B
15. B
16. B
17. D
18. D
19. A
20. A
21. D
22. B
23. C

## Practice Test 6
**Geometry and Measurement**

1. D
2. A
3. C
4. A
5. B
6. B
7. A
8. C
9. D
10. C
11. C
12. B
13. D
14. B
15. C
16. A
17. B
18. D
19. A
20. D

## Practice Test 7
**Problem Solving**

1. C
2. A
3. E
4. C
5. B
6. D
7. E
8. D
9. A
10. A
11. D
12. A
13. A
14. E
15. C
16. B
17. E
18. D
19. A
20. A

## Practice Test 8
**Computation**

1. B
2. A
3. E
4. B
5. E
6. D
7. C
8. C
9. C
10. D
11. C
12. C
13. B
14. D
15. D
16. A
17. B
18. E
19. D
20. D
21. C
22. B
23. D
24. D
25. A